What We Live For,
What We Die For

BOOKS BY SERHIY ZHADAN

IN ENGLISH TRANSLATION

What We Live For, What We Die For
Mesopotamia
Voroshilovgrad
Depeche Mode

What We Live For, What We Die For: Selected Poems

SERHIY ZHADAN

TRANSLATED FROM THE UKRAINIAN BY
VIRLANA TKACZ AND WANDA PHIPPS

FOREWORD BY BOB HOLMAN

YALE UNIVERSITY PRESS ■ NEW HAVEN & LONDON

A MARGELLOS
WORLD REPUBLIC OF LETTERS BOOK

The Margellos World Republic of Letters is dedicated to making literary works from around the globe available in English through translation. It brings to the English-speaking world the work of leading poets, novelists, essayists, philosophers, and playwrights from Europe, Latin America, Africa, Asia, and the Middle East to stimulate international discourse and creative exchange.

English translation copyright © 2019 by Yale University.

The poems in this volume were originally published in Ukrainian in the following collections: *Життя Марії*, Meridian Czernowitz (2015) © Suhrkamp Verlag Berlin; *Ефіопія*, видавництво "Фоліо" (2009) © Serhiy Zhadan; *Марадона*, видавництво "Фоліо" (2007) © Serhiy Zhadan; *Цитатник*, видавництво "Фоліо" (2005) © Suhrkamp Verlag Berlin; *Історія культури початку століття*, видавництво "Часопис 'Критика'" (2003) © Suhrkamp Verlag Berlin; *Балади про війну та відбудову*, видавництво "Кальварія" (2001) © Serhiy Zhadan.

Yale University Press books may be purchased in quantity for educational, business, or promotional use. For information, please e-mail sales.press@yale.edu (U.S. office) or sales@yaleup.co.uk (U.K. office).

Set in Electra and Nobel types by Tseng Information Systems, Inc., Durham, North Carolina.
Printed in the United States of America.

Library of Congress Control Number: 2018956754
ISBN 978-0-300-22336-1 (paper : alk. paper)

A catalogue record for this book is available from the British Library.
This paper meets the requirements of ANSI/NISO Z39.48–1992 (Permanence of Paper).

10 9 8 7 6 5 4 3 2 1

CONTENTS

FOREWORD
Bob Holman

I thought this would be simple enough—here at last! a Horn of Plenty of poems by Serhiy Zhadan, the "Rock-Star poet," "poet laureate of Eastern Ukraine," Ukraine's "most famous counterculture writer," as labeled by the *New York Times*, the *New Yorker*, and the *London Review of Books*.

After all, I have performed with Zhadan in Ukraine, read the English translations at his readings in the United States, and participated in theatricalizations of his words for the Yara Arts Group, the Ukrainian-U.S. theater company led by Virlana Tkacz, one of the superb translators of this volume (the other, Wanda Phipps, is an American poet).

I know and admire Zhadan, love his poetry, and am convinced he's a poet the world should know about—he has the bold straightforwardness and casual surrealism of Vladimir Mayakovsky, and for many he is the contemporary heir to Taras Schevchenko, Ukraine's beloved national poet. Zhadan is also a lone wolf iconoclast, a prolific writer of novels as well as poetry, and deeply committed to Ukrainian freedom and justice movements. He started writing about the New Ukraine (often not so different from the old, as he informs us) when the Soviet Union dissolved. He actively participated in the Orange Revolution and the recent demonstrations at the Maidan, all from his cultural vantage point of the East, where the war zone is now, a place where his pro-Ukrainian views are not the most popular. His political beliefs and big mouth can get him into trouble. He was beaten up by a gang of pro-Russian thugs with a baseball bat at a demonstration in Kharkiv in 2014 and spent a month in the hospital with a broken jaw and concussion. Seems they demanded that he kneel and kiss the Russian flag. "I told them to go fuck themselves," Zhadan posted on Facebook.

But now, in the second month of the Trump regime, a different significance is emerging from this book, one that adds another layer of meaning. Zhadan's poems, which so extraordinarily depict the lives of working-class Ukrainians struggling against an implacable alien machine dedicated to eating their very identities, their *souls* if I can say that, whose road to the future seems blocked at every turn by oligarchs and remnants of a Russian past in which Ukrainians were forced away from their country's heritage, now seem like a game plan for a U.S. citizenry struggling to come to grips with their own demagogic forces hellbent on challenging the foundations of *their* country—freedom of speech, freedom of the press, protection of the poor and newly arrived, etc. His Putin is their Putin. I mean Trump. Put Ukraine's president Viktor Yanukovych in the mix. The list goes on and on.

Zhadan's poetry reveals Ukraine to be a country that is almost as multilayered and diverse as the United States. This is particularly true of the eastern part of the country, where he's from and still lives, in which immigrants from China, Kyrgyzstan, Africa, Mongolia, and all over east Europe work together in a place for which Russian has been the predominant language for over a century. (During the Russian occupation, Ukrainian was suppressed in schools and government facilities. After independence, it was welcome in the streets, and municipalities conducted business in whatever language the people were most comfortable using. Until recently, there was a plurality of Russian speakers, but since Putin's land grab of Crimea and the punishing war in the East, more and more people are choosing to speak Ukrainian. This is the first time I've ever heard of a country switching to another language simply by the will of the people, not via a formal policy. It's estimated at this point that about 54 percent of Ukrainians are claiming Ukrainian as their primary language, marking the first time the country has been majority Ukrainian speaking in over a hundred years.)

Many of Zhadan's poems are persona poems, in which the lives and narratives intertwine and lay out the fabric of the country. "When all this began," "the new situation," "when all this started"—you can find little hints like these in many of Zhadan's poems, especially from his most recent book, *Why I Am Not on Social Media.* Innocuous sounding, these phrases at first seem to refer simply to the story of the person you're reading about: the tattoo artist, the disappeared woman's musician brother, the male social worker who blogs as a Chechen girl, the Chinese Ukrainian drug mule. But gradually it dawns on you that something ominous has happened, that what seems to be a new reality is actually the same old oligarchy, perhaps shifted a bit to emit a false light of hope. You see through the code, catapulted back into the era of samizdat. But these poems are not just about Russia—"the new situation" reads like prophesy after the 2016 U.S. election. Small incidents of racial tension, individual actions of prejudice start to increase and reveal a deep darkness lurking just below the surface, a debilitating inertia that piles up into sadness and fear.

Zhadan's poetry comes direct from the land, from Ukraine itself. It's a *Canterbury Tales* of Ukrainian common people. And who are the common people? Farmers. Soldiers. Drug dealers, contrabanders, street people, youth in all variety, poor students, owners of small businesses, both legal and illegal—in Ukraine there are plenty of each, and it's often difficult to tell the difference. Zhadan is the voice of immigrants. He's spiritual, if guns and sweat and a stand against hypocrisy make one spiritual. He says he's a punk proletariat, and I find no reason to argue with that. He's a moral compass, but never preachy. His is the morality that reads real on the streets. He sees god in your heart, and everyone has their own god. He's the hardest-working poet in the country, but he makes it seem effortless. He's a tender father, with two children; Zhadan was eighteen when his son was born, and the Maria of his collection *The Life of Maria* is now four and a half (he was thirty-six when she was born). It's in *Maria* that he advises us, in a poem about refugees from the war in eastern Ukraine, to "take only what is most important," which turns out to be letters, "every last piece of bad news," and "unedited lists of the dead, // so long that there won't be enough time / to check them for your own name." It is estimated that the ongoing war in Ukraine has created 1.7 million refugees.

In Zhadan's world, the cellist wants to leave his instrument in the middle of the street. But he can't. It matters that when you grow mushrooms in Donbas you get high. And when you "bury friends in the dirt, / like a dog buries a bone," you then "wait for the sky / to become kinder." His world offers an economy between hope and hopelessness, between reality and surreality—but sometimes you don't know which is which.

Here's how it is with Zhadan. One minute he's the front man for the post-punk proletariat band the Dogs and the next he's reading his poems in an art installation. Nothing artsy-fartsy for him, though. As a singer he snarls and swelters, and at the art installation—well, let me describe one I saw, one of the greatest poetry readings I have ever witnessed.

It took place in October 2013 at the Pinchuk Art Center in Kyiv, just a month or so before the demonstrations and two blocks away from the Maidan, where they happened. The exhibit was a group show of Chinese artists, and the piece Zhadan was using for his performance site was "Seeing Is Not an Option" by the artists Sun Yuan and Peng Yu. A thick wire cage, enclosed on top, almost completely filled the 25-by-50-foot room with 10-foot-high ceilings. It fit so tightly into the space that as a single row of spectators ringed it latecomers had to squeeze past behind them. So it was totally claustrophobic outside the cage, but inside the cell—it felt like a bunker—was a long table, maybe 20 feet long, with chairs around it, like a banquet table but plain, more like something found in an office. And the cage was filled with weapons. Hanging on the walls, stacked on the floor, leaning against the wire, guns of every imaginable sort—machine guns, rifles, pistols, assault weapons, bazookas, with a couple of missile launchers for good measure. All oiled and in perfect condition. And knives. Big, thick knives and bayonets, their blades glinting. And grenades and ammo belts. What spectators were faced with was a munitions dump and a table for preparing plans for attack or defense. A war room with the weapons just a reach away.

For the performance, the twenty folding chairs around the table were occupied by men in military fatigues. On the table in front of each was a rifle. Zhadan entered the cage, took his place opposite the table. Opened his sheaf of poems and launched into his poetry. Mid-level businessmen "wipe their stingy tears and runny noses against their / dolce & gabbana, / slurping hennessy / from disposable / cups."

As soon as he started, each man, as if taking part in some kind of ballet theater, choreographed and directed, took hold of his rifle and began to disassemble it piece by piece, element by element, until what had been a rifle was now a carefully laid out collection of parts, like a science experiment—barrel, trigger, stock, sight, scope, etc. There was a ten-second pause, a silence that Zhadan read through: "Catch a glimpse of the place were navigation disappears, / where silence opens wounds on apples." And then, at some kind of internal clue, the men (they were all men) began in unison to reassemble their weapons, each click and clank crackling the air simultaneously till the guns were complete—it took under a minute. " You feel how much the planets strain / to stay in balance as they stream past you," said the poet.

The team then grasped the guns around the barrels, slammed the gun butts down on the ground with a single *thwack*, then hoisted them and passed them along clockwise to the next person, and the entire ballet began again: disassemble, ten seconds' pause, reassemble, thwack on ground, pass left. Zhadan seemed oblivious to the macabre spectacle going on right in front of him, but his poems were mesmerizing and in their own way seemed rooted in the male war dance assembly line. He rarely looked up or broke his rhythm—it was as if his poems were holding their own against this violence. They were a voice of humanness, a song that could be heard over the mechanisms of war. For him, beaches have "bicycles in the sand / and all these preachers on lifeguard towers." The world is a crazy, upside-down place where there is "too much dependence on dictionaries, / on lexemes, and all those diphthongs that dissolve on the tongue." There was even a sense of humor penetrating the mechanical river of weaponry that it seemed would never stop.

And then it did. Twenty men had disassembled and reassembled twenty rifles twenty times in just over twenty minutes. Zhadan's reading ended then too, perfectly timed: life is "just short enough to be told in one sitting / and too depressing to share with others." The audience didn't know what to do. Applause seemed inappropriate. Zhadan straightened his papers and made for the door. As he strode out there was no room for well-wishers to intervene. He just headed out into the night. I saw a couple of audience members try to enter the cage for a firsthand look at the guns and knives and bombs. Of course they were not allowed in. In a dictatorship, where is the jail and where is freedom?

Here in these poems is all that we've been waiting for: a voice that tells us everything we've never wanted to know. Even if we're not ready for it, we cannot refuse to understand. The job of the poet is to turn words into worlds. It is what we live for, what we die for. Welcome the work of a master poet, now in English, the poetry of Serhiy Zhadan.

New York City, March 1, 2017

What We Live For,
What We Die For

Why I'm Not on Social Media (2015)

NEEDLE

Anton, thirty-two years old,
status includes living with his parents.
Orthodox, but doesn't attend church,
university graduate, studied English.
Worked as a tattoo artist, had a signature style,
if you can call it that.
Many a local passed under
his sharp needle and skillful hand.

When all this began, he talked a lot about
politics and history, started going to rallies,
argued with friends.
Friends took offense, clients disappeared.
They were afraid, didn't understand, left town.

You truly experience a person, touching them with a needle.
A needle pricks; a needle stitches. Under its warm
metal the texture of female skin becomes so supple
and the radiant canvas of male skin so tough.
Piercing through a person's outer membrane,
you release velvety drops of blood, carve out
angels' wings on the submissive surface of the world.
Go carve them, tattoo artist; we are called
to fill this world with meaning, with color.

Carve this shell, tattoo artist, which hides souls and disease—
what we live for, what we die for.

Someone said he was shot at a roadblock
one morning, weapon in hand, somehow accidentally—
no one really knows why.
He was buried in a mass grave—that's how they were all buried.
His personal effects were turned over to his parents.
His status was never updated.

One day some bastard
will definitely write heroic poems about this.
One day another bastard
will say there's no reason to write about this at all.

SEARCH

I searched for her for a long time. She changed her number,
left town, wasn't on Facebook.
I couldn't find her through friends
or through members of her church.
Then she wrote, describing what she was up to:
her journey, the new situation, and how she was getting used to it.

She wrote about her brother; actually, I think that's why she wrote—
to tell us about her brother and his death.
I wasn't the only person she turned to,
I couldn't have been the first.
She wrote too calmly.
She wrote, they were all caught in one round of fire.
Then some of them returned
to recover the dead. Or rather what was left
of them. The legs were the biggest problem. Everybody
needs two legs. That's how they assembled them—
so each had two legs. It was best if they were both
about the same size.

Her brother was a musician. He had a good guitar,
which people constantly borrowed.
"What should I do with it now?" she asked.
"I picked it up and tried to play, but only cut my fingers on the strings.
It was very painful. It still hurts."

SECT

Andrew and Paul were Adventists and students.
Their father, a businessman, supported the community.
They were used to seeing the church
as part of their lives:
they were there every day, helping with
renovations, posting photos on the Net,
thanking people for their support.

In times of peace, they were just considered members of a sect,
but when all this started, a hunt for them
was organized. Some left, others hid.
But the two brothers were caught. They were held in a basement,
forced to bury the dead, dig graves.
They wanted to buy their freedom, were afraid and cried.
They were taken to another hole. Then they were
forgotten, as if they had simply never existed.
They sat in a basement with no light and listened to the dark.
At first they prayed, then they stopped—
and became ashamed of themselves.

You lose your faith when
you lose the possibility
of dying for it. What's faith
to someone who's seen how things really are?

Why believe in something that has
no meaning for you?
No one says anything about what happened to the saints
who bore stigmata on their bodies. What happened
to those stigmata? Did they close at night like roses?
Did they bleed for a long time,
heal, or hurt under the bandages?
Men with eyes blinded by darkness
came to the hospital to have the bandages changed.
They clenched their teeth when the nurse tore
the dry bandages from their wounds and fresh blood
rose on the blackened skin. They asked for
any kind of painkillers.
But there is no painkiller for what hurts them —
pills for that don't exist.

CHECHEN GIRL

Yuriy,
already past forty,
a social worker,
studied history.
He sits on the internet
researching tattered pages of history.
Writes a blog using the alias "Chechen Girl."
He made up this woman sniper,
now lives through her.

He writes about her faith,
writes about her doubts,
writes about her sensitivity,
carves notches on the butt of her rifle:

here is—the enemy-father,
here is—the enemy-son,
here—the holy ghost, also an enemy,
worth mentioning
in the general list
of those to be executed,
whom the invisible sniper
requests in her prayers.

The world's a postal package
fastened with barbed wire.
Tear it open, and out of
children's shirts and towels,
black frogs and snakes
crawl out.

We will never know
who stood in the riled-up crowds,
ready to tear the fragile fabric
of someone else's flesh.
We will never know
who was not in those crowds.

To guide you down
night roads
between grass and coal,
stepping silently
in lightweight sneakers,
to lead you to fresh springs,
avoiding paths well trodden
by cattle,
then leaving you bread for breakfast,
wrapped in
the enemy's colors.

In the morning
he reads what he wrote.

Sometimes he adds something.
Sometimes he corrects things.
He shaves with an old razor
and nicks his skin.

But there is no blood.
There's none at all.
Just as there is no death.

PSYCHO

"He's sorry for the city," he says. "It will be destroyed.
Like Sodom and Gomorrah," he adds.

His brother is confined to a psychiatric ward.
A few days ago the separatists took over the building.
They placed a mine launcher in the yard.

He visits his brother. They sit on the bench under the branches
of an apple tree. They look alike—both in tracksuits,
both with short haircuts. One holds a cell phone,
even though there is no service in the city.

The separatists pay no attention to the brothers.
And the brothers pay no attention to them.

When he was a child, he was ashamed of his brother, never spoke
about him, never took him anywhere. You know
how it is when there is a psycho in the family. Your father is normal,
your mother is normal, and you are normal, but there is
one psycho. A real psycho. A psycho. In your family.
That means you're also suspect.

When he grew up, he stopped paying attention to his brother.
As if he didn't exist. Like when you are walking down a street

and notice something unpleasant in your peripheral vision,
something that provokes fear or disgust: for instance,
a dead animal, but you know
if you don't look at it, then it doesn't exist
and everything's all right.

So now they are sitting together, silently,
and no one pays any attention to them. As if they
don't exist. There must be many others —
who didn't manage to escape,
who lie on the side of the road
like roadkill.

The management of the ward fled a long time ago.
A few cleaning ladies are taking care of the sick.
Old women who have worked here
all their lives. Six or seven of them.
Not too bad, I guess, for a city of over a million.

PILLAGER

Bad family history,
history like that winds up on the morning news.
His old man froze in December on an empty tram.
His mother had problems with sugar.
He dropped out of trade school after two years,
his throat burned by iodine,
his ear damaged by a metal pipe.

What did you dream about all those years?
What did you want?

Everything he wanted was
in the closest shopping mall.
Destroying it was like
breaking the seals on a papal bull.

"I never," he wrote, "had enough money
to buy what I really wanted. I always
had to put it off till better times.
But now I understand that better times
will never come.

"You were born here too.
You know how it is.

Repeat after me:
life is cruel and unfair,
life is hopeless and short,
life is depressing and gutless.
He who has nothing
gets nothing.
He who has nothing to lose
loses nothing."

It's been a long time since anyone expected
better times here. A quiet death here is
like a woman with
a good heart, but bad lungs—
you live with her because you love her,
but you'll die because you lived with her.

"Thanks for writing," he says,
"thanks for writing."
"It's nothing," I answer.
And really—it is nothing.

HEADPHONES

Sasha, a quiet drunk, an esoteric, a poet,
spent the entire summer in the city.
When the shooting began, he was surprised —
started watching the news, then stopped.
He walks around the city with headphones on,
listening to golden oldies,
as he stumbles into burned-out cars,
blown-up bodies.

What will survive from the history
of the world in which we lived
will be the words and music of a few geniuses
who desperately tried to warn us,
tried to explain, but failed to explain anything
or save anyone;
these geniuses lie in cemeteries
and out of their ribcages
grow flowers and grass.
Nothing else will remain —
only their music and songs, a voice
that forces you to love.

You can choose to never turn off this music.
Listen to the cosmos, shut your eyes.

Think about whales in the ocean at night.
Hear nothing else.
See nothing else.
Feel nothing else.
Except, of course, for the smell,
the smell of corpses.

CHAPLAIN

Ihor, a chaplain, thirty years old,
doesn't shave so he'll look older.
Everyone wants to look mature, more serious,
especially thirty-year-olds.
You can lose yourself at that age.
It's a dangerous age, even for chaplains.

It's strange to hear the confessions of men,
who stubbornly and consistently break all
of the Lord's commandments. Deaf and angry,
they brand skin with red-hot metal,
burn lips with tobacco, smoke
in the wind.
Cigarette butts fall on the wet grass—
with little crucifixes, holy pictures,
and gun grease under their fingernails,
they turn off their phones
and go to confess.

They tell him their secrets, share their troubles.
He'd rather not listen, but what can he do?
Every sin is like a stone from the seashore.
Angry men place these stones in his hand—
everyone places a warm stone, long carried in their pocket.

The chaplain has bags filled with these stones,
which he can hardly move.
But they still keep on coming and coming,
bringing their stones,
handing them to him,
as if they were things of great importance.

Constantly, for days on end,
they finish smoking, joke, get in line,
afraid they're too late and won't get their turn.

Everyone will get their turn.
No one will be too late.

SPY

Volodya, twenty-five years old,
a doctor, a psychologist,
has a video blog, teaches the proper
attitudes for life,
how to find joy in the everyday;
he explains the meaning of simple words,
dispels negative energy,
as if it were heavy river sand.

Two months ago he was taken prisoner.
They found his camera and accused him of spying.
There's no hope for his release; he will sit there
till Judgment Day.

He lies in a concrete cell, on a mattress,
covered with a blanket, dressed in someone else's sweater
with bloodstains. He lies next to someone
so dark, he's afraid to even glance
in his direction. He lies there and the dark one gets to him:

Your everyday things, spy,
are underwear and day-old bread.
But the Lord's will, spy,
is a scratchy blanket that smells of rain.
Hide under it, oh spy, smell it, stare at it.

Spy on your homeland, try to see what
it is trying so hard to hide from you,
what it will never share; stare into the light in the crack,
where justice is meted out.

The holy family hides
behind the doors of an unheated building.
The hole in the broken door is stuffed with the scratchy blanket.
Now how can we understand the meaning of
simple words and not complain about the lack
of heat, or the disturbing light?

The time will come when they will call even you, spy.
They will call all of us, with our things, our blankets
and bits of pain.
We will go off into the blue snow,
we will go off into the red night,
we will go toward the light of a crack in the heavens,
we will hasten to Judgment Day.
Judge us, judge us, oh judges, deprived of hope,
judge us, judge us, oh judges, and send us
to rehabilitation camps.

Rehabilitated, frightened,
we speak simple words.
We wolf down hot snow with dry mouths.
We grab the last of the snow,
which is like gold.

RHINOCEROS

For half a year she's been holding on.
For half a year she's been staring at death,
like at a rhinoceros in a zoo —
dark folds,
heavy breathing.
She is afraid but doesn't look away,
doesn't shut her eyes.

It's frightening, very frightening.
And it should be.
Death is frightening, it scares you.
It's frightening to smell the stench of a blood moon.
It's frightening to see how history is made.

Half a year ago everything was totally different.
Half a year ago everyone was different.
No one was afraid of stars falling
over the reservoir.
No one paid attention to the smoke
that rose through the cracks in the dark ground.

At night in the middle of the street,
in the noise and the headlights,
between death and love,

she burrows her face into his shoulder,
pounds him desperately with her fists,
cries and screams in the dark.
"I don't want to see all of this," she says,
"I can't carry all of this inside me.
Why do I need all this death?
Where should I put it?"

Where to put all this death?
Strap it to our backs
the way Gypsies carry their children:
no one loves it
and it loves no one.
There is so little love,
love is so fragile.

Cry and shatter the dark with your warm hands.
Cry but don't move away from him even a step.
The world will never be what it was before.
We will never let it be
like it was before.

There are fewer and fewer lit windows on the empty street.
There are fewer and fewer people strolling
by the store windows.
Fields and rivers grow still in the hell of this autumn mist.
The fires go out in the rain.
The cities freeze in the night.

Life of Maria (2015)

"Where are you coming from, dark caravan, you flock of birds?"
"We once lived in a city that no longer exists.
We have come here tired and ready to submit.
Chaplain, tell your people, there's no one left to kill.

"Our city was built of stone and steel.
Now we are each left holding only one bag,
A suitcase filled with ashes, gathered under fire.
Now we smell the burning even in our dreams.

"The women of our city were sound as a bell and carefree.
At night their fingers reached down into the void.
The city springs ran deep, deep as a well.
The churches were grand. We burned them ourselves.

"Gravestones will tell our stories best.
Chaplain, can you just talk to us?
Brace us with your love.
Confession is part of your job.

"Tell us, why did they burn our city down?
Tell us they did not mean to do it.
Tell us the guilty will be punished, Chaplain.
Tell us anything that's not on the news."

"Well, I can only tell you about the losses.
Surely a final reckoning awaits the guilty.
But it awaits the innocent as well and
even those who had nothing to do with this.

"How did you end up with these dark fleeing masses?
You should have read the prophets more carefully.
You should have avoided the road that leads to hell.
The people cannot bear to see faith in action.

"Remember what the prophets said about pain and long-suffering,
about the birds that fall from the sky like stones on a city?
That's when the losses really start.
Where they end, you can't even imagine.

"How are we different? As consonants from vowels.
Everyone can accept a death that's not their own.
In this life no one avoids the final reckoning.
That's what I tell people when there's nothing left to say.

"I don't know anything about inevitable penance.
I don't know where and how you should live.
I can only speak of what's inside us.
You must realize how unlucky we've all been."

"TAKE ONLY WHAT IS MOST IMPORTANT"

Take only what is most important. Take the letters.
Take only what you can carry.
Take the icons and the embroidery, take the silver,
Take the wooden crucifix and the golden replicas.

Take some bread, the vegetables from the garden, then leave.
We will never return again.
We will never see our city again.
Take the letters, all of them, every last piece of bad news.

We will never see our corner store again.
We will never drink from that dry well again.
We will never see familiar faces again.
We are refugees. We'll run all night.

We will run past fields of sunflowers.
We will run from dogs, rest with cows.
We'll scoop up water with our bare hands,
sit waiting in camps, annoying the dragons of war.

You will not return, and friends will never come back.
There will be no smoky kitchens, no usual jobs,
There will be no dreamy lights in sleepy towns,
no green valleys, no suburban wastelands.

The sun will be a smudge on the window of a cheap train,
rushing past cholera pits covered with lime.
There will be blood on women's heels,
tired guards on borderlands covered with snow,

a postman with empty bags shot down,
a priest with a hapless smile hung by his ribs,
the quiet of a cemetery, the noise of a command post,
and unedited lists of the dead,

so long that there won't be enough time
to check them for your own name.

"YOU CAN FIND JUST ABOUT EVERYTHING
DOWN AT THE TRAIN STATION"

You can find just about everything down at the train station:
morning bird songs, bursts of sunshine,
dark dew, and tar-covered railroad ties.
The first to leave were the merchants,
then shrewd unnoticed vagrants, invisible drifters,
trained security guards, night military cadets.

Then the jewelers left, then the lawyers,
then the bankers, to avoid the barricades.
Though who would complain about bankers?
Then the astronomers left, after that the poets.
The wind sweeps the winter newspapers.
Children wear crosses around their necks and green berets.

Then the mothers left, and girls who were engaged,
then students—both learned and ignorant
(homesick, with a taste for honey and roasts).
Tragic events are first of all simply events—
all to be remembered in times of sorrow and hopelessness.

Only you and I are left.
Because the possibility of peace, or war,
is no reason to run with the mob.

Fervent Christians and hopeless bandits—
it's so hard to put us to sleep and hard to wake us.
Nothing will prevent us from killing each other now.

I am just like you: there's bristle on my chin, like yours.
We share the same eternal tan, wives just as cold,
burns and scars, and spiderwebs of wrinkles.
We are just as offended at God for injustice,
ready to grab every opportunity
to display our steadfastness, to show off our wit.

Go ahead, kill me for our mutual passions,
kill me for all that we were once taught,
wake me in the middle of the night with heavy keys.
I will kill you too,
remembering your every fault.
And if I can't—I'll ask you for advice.

I too will have no doubt and will not waver.
I'll pay off your debts, fulfill your expectations.
The last wish is a delight because it is the last.
Where did your journey begin, where will it end?
You were always one of them, and you still are, to this day.
You can meet just about anyone at these train stations.

As long as the warm weather lasts in town,
past the whistle of the locomotives and birds,

past the voices of the market poor at night,
as long as any people are left behind,
let all the railroad stations stay open,
let dreamy villagers share bread and milk,
let their journey be easy, let them be rescued in time.

"SO I THROW DOWN MY WEAPON AND START TO CRAWL"

So I throw down my weapon and start to crawl,
crawl away from something I never believed in,
I crawl avoiding roads and swamps,
crawl past dead patrols and bombed-out command posts.

I crawl past borders, past fortified bridges,
across my country—vast and useless.
This will take a long time, but I have time to kill,
so what difference does it make what I crawl past?

Every night used to flow by slowly, like a river.
Every morning was anticipated like a gift.
Now I mouth words of thanks and disdain,
sitting in a darkness—warm and sticky like the inside of a sheep's belly.

The dead speak from under the earth, the saints from the heavens above.
In their distance there is compassion and balance.
Even if I have nowhere to run—
the blasted earth will protect this deserter.

What lies in your heart, my country, what is on your mind?
I don't even know what colors are used to sew our banners.
Demons stand at my back—untrustworthy but real,
reproaching me, reminding me of my oath.

When I forget all this and escape,
when I stop dreaming of the dead floating down rivers,
when I see in each of the dead only death,
when my voice and my conscience are clear,

when I am no longer afraid of the dark,
when each breath is filled with resonance,
I too will speak, I will speak to everyone,
I will speak about the living and the dead.

Ten thousand dead listen under the earth.
Ten thousand saints listen overhead.
The voices of the dead are distant and angry.
The voices of the saints are also angry and smell of fresh-cut grass.

People look out of their windows,
run out of their warm homes.
It will be summer in the city
as the deserter returns.

He avoids conversations,
like the devil.
He doesn't remember addresses
or recognize family members.

And his family
returns home
but does not recognize him,
does not recognize him.

The dark shattered wicked winter
silence waits at the door like death.
What will remain of this winter
will be the words and how you said them.

All our troubles will be blamed on them.
They will be quoted and picked apart.
But I will just love them
and remember them.

I will remember the sky and how high it seemed.
I will remember cities suddenly startled by screams.
History becomes simple and clear
when I decide to fill it with laughter.

Remember the snow on your lashes,
remember the sun, searing, like a burn.
Children born after these snowstorms
will recognize this land by touch.

They will recognize its water by taste,
they will recognize the color of its wheat,
they will love its dry spells and storms,
they will even love its hospitals and prisons.

I will remember the chill under our nails,
the fire that dried out our throats,
your last moves in the middle of the night—
light, hesitant, final.

Children born under those stars
and named after the dead,
will exude wisdom in each breath,
while talking to enemies and thieves.

They will be stubborn and sure of themselves,
as if their future held no death,
as if their past held no rage.
They will remember everything that's been forgotten.

They will make their way in night storms,
overcoming hurdles and obstacles.
They can handle it, try and teach them
to believe, to love and to remember.

Remember all that they carry with them:
the grass blackened by snow,
the sky over scorched heads,
the earth under tired feet.

"ALL NIGHT LONG SHE SINGS IN HER ROOM"

All night long she sings in her room,
her fingers sticky with blood and cotton candy.
Grief scorches her veins from the inside,
ship horns scream like birds.
Lord, protect the queen of our hit parade.

All morning long she packs her bags.
She has three days before her visa expires.
She has a tank full of gas
and a long list of thanks to the Lord
with lots of interesting material
for criminal investigators.

No one prevents her from leaving today
to appear unexpectedly at night
moving toward the abyss.
An empty hostel. Top bunk.
Dog-eared phone book,
where all the local numbers
now have international codes.

No one stops her from speaking clearly and simply,
as she writes her notes, sometimes slipping into prose,
explaining what happened,

why the exhaustion, why she's grown old.
No one stops her,
but no one asks her either.

What can you ask a person whose heart is full of loss,
in her soul—parting and tenderness,
in her hand—a grenade,
in her lungs—cold silvery ice floes,
in her memory—sailors who went down with their ship.
Even her heart has a museum catalogue number.

I know everything and don't stand in her way.
I consider everything, step aside, and don't stop her.
The drawing on her skin,
the sharp shoulders,
twenty minutes to collect her things—
dry wine of this year's vintage.

All evening long she sits in a black sweater.
Her movements are clear, her desire persistent.
All week long in song and confession,
all winter long awaiting the flood.
All of her life lived so she won't fear death.

CELLIST

The cellist drags
his wooden instrument,
stops
to catch his breath,
barely holding himself up,
then slowly shuffles
down the cobblestones.
They start yelling
right in his face,
their curses come
from all sides.

Men gather,
women stare,
children throw golden
slivers of pavement at him
like lemons.

He has never heard
such harsh words.
It's not his fault
that he must play
this cursed funeral music.
It's not his fault,

he can't just leave his instrument
in the middle of the street.
How can he
explain it to them?

A shout shatters the air
then breaks into a lament.
Soon blood will spill,
soon tears will flow.

Men scowl,
women scream,
children will remember the look of this sky
to the end of
their days.

Then when they reach
the edge of town and pause
on a hill, he places
his instrument on the ground,
takes out his bow,
embraces the lacquered wood,
hangs over it,
no strength left to let it go,
his movements heavy,
his palms start to bleed.
Then

men cry,
women's hearts flutter,
and in the clenched fists
of the children pearls
of music start to seed.

Ethiopia (2009)

"NEITHER THE SMALLEST GIRL IN CHINATOWN"

Neither the smallest girl in Chinatown
nor old Baptists in the cold churches of Manhattan
can imagine the starlight that falls into our chimneys
and the emerald green of the garlic leaves
that grow on our soccer fields.

Here the ocean, without beginning or end,
runs over the shore lined with Chinese food stands,
while thousands of sperm whales hide in the silt and sand,
forever separating me from the land
I loved.

Here black trees in the cold snow,
like women from Africa wrapped in white sheets,
are lined with birds on each limb,
birds screeching of emigration,
birds singing of exile.

Here I am
every night
in dreams,
loading my ship with stars and grain,
filling the hold with rum and hemlock,
warming the old engines
like ancient stoves.

The Lord Almighty will summon us soon,
reversing the currents of the ocean, flinging us into the dark.
Cry for me,
O blind seaweed of America,
as only you can,
as only you can.

Maradona (2007)

THE MUSHROOMS OF DONBAS

In spring Donbas disappears in the fog, and the sun hides behind heaps of earth.
So you need to know where you're going,
you need to know the man who can make the arrangements.

This man was a worker in the former pumping station,
worn down by alcohol.
When we met, he said, "We, the workers of the pumping station,
were always considered the elite of the proletariat, yeah, the elite.
When everything fell the fuck apart, many
just threw up their hands. But not us, the workers
of the pumping station.
We organized an independent union,
took over three buildings of the former plant
and started growing mushrooms there."

"Mushrooms?" I couldn't believe it.
"Yes. Mushrooms. We wanted to grow cactus with mescaline, but
cactus won't grow here in Donbas.

"You know what's important when you grow mushrooms?
It's important to get high, that's right, friend—it's important to get high.
We get high, believe me, even now we have to get high. Maybe it's because
we are the elite of the proletariat.

"And so—we take over three buildings and start our mushrooms.
Well, there's the joy of work, elbow grease,
you know—the heady feeling of work accomplished.
And what's more important—everyone gets high! Everyone's high even without
  mushrooms!

"The problems began a few months later. This is gangland
territory, you know, recently a gas station was burned down,
they were so eager to burn it down, they didn't even manage to
fill up—so of course the police caught them.
And so one gang decides to take us on, to take away
our mushrooms, can you believe it? I think in our place anyone else
would have bent over, that's the way it is—everyone bends here,
according to the social hierarchy.

"But we get together and think, well, mushrooms—this is a good thing,
it's not a matter of mushrooms, or elbow grease,
or even the pumping station, although this was one of the arguments.
We just thought, they are coming up, they will grow,
our mushrooms will grow, you could say they'll ripen to harvest
and what are we going to tell our children, how are we going to look them in the eye?
There are things you have to answer for, things
you can't just let go.
You are responsible for your own penicillin
and I am responsible for mine.

"So we fought for our mushroom plantations. That is where
we beat them. And when they fell on the warm hearts of the mushrooms,
we thought—

"Everything that you make with your hands works for you.
Everything that reaches your conscience beats
in rhythm with your heart.
We stayed here, so that it wouldn't be far
for our children to visit our graves.
This is our island of freedom,
our expanded
village consciousness.
Penicillin and Kalashnikovs—two symbols of struggle,
the Castro of Donbas leads the partisans
through the fog-covered mushroom plantations
to the Azov Sea.

"You know," he told me, "at night, when everyone falls asleep
and the dark land sucks up the fog,
I feel how the earth moves around the sun, even in my dreams
I listen and hear how they grow—

"the mushrooms of Donbas, silent chimeras of the night,
emerging out of the emptiness, growing out of hard coal,
till hearts stand still, like elevators in buildings at night,
the mushrooms of Donbas grow and grow, never letting the discouraged
and condemned die of grief,

because, man, as long as we're together,
there's someone to dig up this earth,
and find in its warm innards
the black stuff of death,
the black stuff of life."

LUKOIL

When easter arrives the sky becomes kinder,
but everyone becomes more intense—you know, easter is resurrection day,
when the dead start to turn in the ground,
breaking up the cold clay with their elbows.
I've had to bury friends.
I know what it's like to bury friends in the dirt,
like a dog buries a bone,
and wait for the sky
                to become kinder.

There are social groups
for whom such rituals are very important,
I mean, first of all, mid-level businessmen.
Everyone has seen
the sorrow that envelops these regional
representatives of russian gas companies
when they descend on the vast
cemetery fields, to bury
one more brother shot through the lungs;

everyone has heard their loud heartbeats
when they stand near the coffin
and wipe their stingy tears and runny noses against their
dolce & gabbana,

slurping hennessy

    from disposable

        cups.

"So, Kolia," they say, "here's your payoff.
In the great field of offshore business
we fall into cold pools of oblivion,
like wild autumn geese with buckshot in our livers."

"So," they ask, "when we
send off our brother
on his long journey
into the radiant Valhalla of Lukoil,
who will accompany him
through the dark caverns of purgatory?"

"Bitches," they all say, "bitches
he'll need bitches,
good bitches
expensive ones, without bad habits,
they will warm him in the winter,
they will chill his blood in the spring,
on his left will lie a platinum blonde,
on his right will lie a platinum blonde,
and he won't even notice he's dead.

Oh, death is a territory where

        our credit won't reach.

Death is the territory of oil,
                    let it cleanse his sins.
We'll place his weapons at his feet, as well as gold,
furs, and finely ground pepper.
In his left hand we will place his newest nokia,
and in his right an indulgence from Jerusalem.
But the main thing's the bitches,
two bitches, the main thing's two platinum bitches."
"Yes, that's the main thing," everyone agrees.
"The main thing's the bitches," they agree.
"The main-main thing," adds Kolia from the casket.

We're all sentimental at easter time.
We stand and wait for the dead
to rise and come to us from the hereafter.
When you bury friends,
you become more interested in death.

On the third day as they flank
the doors of the morgue, on the morning of the third day
he conquers death through death, and walks out
from the crematorium; he sees
that they have all fallen asleep, exhausted
from the three-day drinking spree,
sprawled out on the grass,
in vomit-covered
dolce & gabbana.

Then quietly,

               so as not to wake them up,

he takes from one of them

the charger for a nokia,

and returns

to hell

to his

blondes.

UkSSR (2004)

CONTRABAND

In a broken seat, ripped out of a truck,
looking at clouds overhead
since early morning
sits the young god of European contraband,
wrapped in a down jacket,
listening to a Gypsy melody play on a stolen cell phone.

My countrymen, winter has come to our land
and oil shines in cellars, fish fall asleep in reservoirs,
churches and train stations are heated only by long conversations—
there is always more warmth in winter voices than sense.

Tear the tanned leather of shearlings and bomber jackets;
as long as we know every saint
on our border by name,
countrymen, our sons can't be hurt by knives or bullets
or carried off by the current or blown away by the north wind.

Snow in the mountain pass,
the bitches at customs
will take your weapons,
will take your drugs.
You will stand like a ghost in the fog, gold scattered about—
Where now, Lord, where are your Carpathians?

Who should I spend the night with in these fields without snow?
How can I cross to the other side; how can I stand
the fury which fills me since you abandoned me?—
Lord, pull me out from this shit,
if you can see me in this fog.

Wandering sun, roll through our quiet days,
come, my joy, warm yourself with fire and wine.
While you suffer winter is passing,
there's only our heat—nothing else
between you and me—only a river
filled with fish and water.

. . . not to wake her up,
carefully stepping over the things she left,
books and clothes, fragments of a May night
warm as the air; stepping over these in the silence
where walls, windows, stairways, and stagnant darkness
settle in the dregs;
stepping closer to the wet, fresh shutters,
where the solitude of plants and trees begins,
                    warmed by their own growth,
hearths of homes heated by the breath of entire provinces,
the breath of a country, a hot May night on the plains,
deep viscous ground actively expanding
toward its surface;
stepping over the grass, you feel how much the planets strain
to stay in balance as they stream past you,
the entire atmosphere, which accompanies you,
all the darkness of the world, the order of all things
the measure and imperceptible drift of the objects
inside themselves; your moment expands,
but not enough to encompass
this parting in May and the alarming heat of the factories.

To begin from a different place each time,
to emerge every time from the black nothingness toward voices

and the breath of those you share life with,
touching all the scars and veins on the body of your country,
all the bends in the twigs that keep their balance,
touching the warm air currents that spread over you,
washing out dreams from hearts,
so that by morning she no longer remembers
what she dreamt that night.

Light spilling from atom to atom,
straightening the roots and the stems that give them height,
dragging the slippery sap filled with bitterness
along the railroad tracks, pulling along
swallows and insects, chimneys and antennae—
the trees reach with their bodies toward those places,
where our atmosphere breaks off
and where nothingness begins,
almost reaching that point where twilight appears,
where only silence is strewn and rain forms.
And before crossing that boundary, before landing on the other side of air,
before finally untangling themselves from the dense May background
they suddenly think that even the smallest motion,
the smallest shudder of a wet twig will not go unpunished,
for stirring up the air, displacing space,
and awakening her from her dream.
This is what stops them . . .

. . . remember how winter began in your town,
how everyone who dared to stay and live
lived, clinging to the snow and air,
lived, struggling to stay alive;
how all your friends
tried to turn the tides of time away from you
but the first wave swept over them,
scorching them on the inside, sending them reeling around the world,
how each had his back broken by the morning rays,
wanting to do what he wanted,
but not knowing how yet.

To get over a difficult winter, climb out of a deep depression on long railroad cars;
stories you can't unravel,
love you can't get used to;
in fleeting shadows, in tunnels, canals,
depots, oil tankers;
What—tell me—what can I do without you
in this emptiness filled
with your absence, your unwritten letters,
our unspoken conversations, unseen heavens,
imperceptible warmth, nonexistent god;
it turns out I don't have my own habits,
all our habits were shared;

anyway, what kind of habits can you have in this snow,
which I can't get used to.

How did this winter begin?—
there they lay in bed,
sleeping through classes,
losing the battle,
overhead only roof and sky,
no one knows which they need more now.

Barges bound for Yugoslavia float by,
angels repair the buoys.
And the trees stretch upward,
to be closer to him when he calls.

In the morning the vegetables are brought into town
and the sand glows gold in the sun,
on the teeth and shirts of the workers,
mixed with blood and vermouth.

You'll never be free of these criminals,
never get used to this country,
never forget about the inevitability of death,
never remember her explanations.

"THE HOT HEART OF THE YEAR IS BURNING"

The hot heart of the year is burning,
forged—link by link—
by hard coals from under the roots of the forest,
iron blades push through sand and coal,
grow together at the core.

At the very center, right between June and July,
in quiet urban alleys with their vegetable stands,
where you see lindens and abandoned cars fade in the shadow,
you will pass through that mercurial time between seasons
that briefly hesitates, but can turn
in either direction;
out of this—deepest valley—
there are two paths, lightly bouncing,
you can move against the current, breaking through to winter and the source,
when everything did not seem so set,
when you could still change everything;

someone spreads fragrant algae
on the waters of your memory,
spreads smoke, stones, and algae,
and you inhale
the smoke,
enraptured.

The middle of the year—a river in the lowlands, right before the delta,
when the foreign evocative salty
smell of seawater breaks upstream,
filling the pores of the river;
then if you want you can
feel the icy streams of your future,
see what's ahead beyond the closest hills,
catch a glimpse of the place where navigation disappears,
where silence opens wounds on apples,
where nothing begins
without your presence.

THE LORD SYMPATHIZES WITH OUTSIDERS

I looked out at the sea and understood everything—
for three days I had been wandering up and down the empty shore,
walking out into the wetlands where raindrops hung
and fell, you know, into those wetlands, and swam
there like fish, for three days I saw the golden light of diners, motels,
and harbor eateries packed with workers in
white T-shirts who drowned in alcohol as their sweet saliva
colored their liquor pink,

this is what I think—
I think Jesus was a red, he made
all this up on purpose so you would suffer,
as you run into all the mistakes in his blueprints,
he seems to be saying on purpose—
Look, he says to you,
here is your heart, here is her heart, do you hear how they beat?
You're alive, as long as you listen to all the sounds and movements deep under your skin,
you're alive, as long as you see what's happening there—
inside of things or objects rising up beneath the surface.

And then I thought, you know—all these bicycles in the sand
and all these preachers on lifeguard towers—
when you wade far out into the water and preach to all
the jellyfish and flying fish, lecturing to them, as they
patiently swim around you, explaining

to them the dimmest and most terrifying entries in your
dictionary, telling them

that Jesus was a red, with all his leftist tricks
like walking on water, all his apostles —
engineers from the local tech, who gathered at the factory
for their last supper, all those golden threads in your sweater
and scabs on your knees,

Jesus was definitely red, he counted on
the communist principles of bird flight,
and all the rest so that you would suffer,
listening to the heartbeat of trees and bicycles,
to the conversations of foremen, whose tongues are washed
down with cool liquor, like new chrome.

The green grass which will grow on these foundations,
the green grass which no one knows yet, the green
grass around which the heavens spin,
grass — green and damp is the reason for
everything;

this girl has such narrow veins that sometimes
her blood can't push through them;
can you hear her heart in the winter when skin dries like a river?
her heart beats slower now;
this means that she is either asleep
or simply very calm.

SWEET PEPPERS

Walking through the supermarket at night
past the green flash of salads,
behind the two teens holding hands —
the girl picks out lemons and sweet peppers
and lets the boy hold them, then laughs and puts them back.
It's ten to ten; before this they argued
for a long time, she wanted to leave, he convinced her to stay;
pockets full of green stuff,
gold Assyrian coins, painkillers,
sweet love, enchanted green peppers.

Take us out, come on, take us out, the dank soul, every dead fruit, the blood of
strawberries, and fish killed by old ship propellers in southern states, minced
with earrings and British punk pins, their gills stuffed with
caffeine, black disease, turning away from the green light, they groan as if begging,

Take us out from here, come on, take us out to the nearest bus stop, to the nearest
gas station, to the nearest cool ocean, they seem to signal, bending
their dank souls, till the propellers in the night skies above the supermarket
wreck the juicy air, and the caffeine stains your fingernails,

Take us out, well come on, hide the warm green flashes in your pockets, place silver
    and gold coins under your tongue, take us to the nearest hiding place, to the nearest
    stadium,
blood for blood, the Lord calls us, moving his fins.

Since I won't ever be able to hold anyone
the way he holds her, I can't simply pass by
all this still life; I hesitated too long,
didn't have the strength to move, so now I have to follow them.

You must know what awaits them, right? Where you are now, where
you wound up, you can predict everything—two or three more years of golden
teenage swooning in the August grass, squandering coins on all kinds of
poisons and that's it—memory fills the place in you once occupied by tenderness.

Since I won't ever be able to be afraid for anyone
the way she is afraid for him, I won't ever be able to give
anything to anyone with the ease with which she places
the warm lemons in his hands;
I will follow them farther
through the long exhausting twilight of the supermarket,
with yellow grass underfoot,
dead fish in hand,
warming its heart
with my breath,
warming my breath
with its heart.

DICTIONARIES IN THE SERVICE OF THE CHURCH

It so happened that the woman he loved decided to
leave his country, simply saying one day,
you know, I have to go, we still have a couple of months,
you can call me. all right, he said, all right,
and then? then what? she asked. then what
will happen to your number? will they take it away from you or will you
give it to someone else? you know what I mean? who will pick up
the phone when I call you in a couple of months?

Well, I don't know, she said; the number
will be destroyed. What do you mean destroyed? look—they'll take it
and destroy it. and what then? then? then nothing:
I will leave this country, and will be busy doing something
like reading, traveling, maybe praying. and me?
and you? well, you can also pray, if you have the time.

All right, he said, that's what I will do—I will learn
some prayers and I will pray. I wonder,
she said, I wonder, what will you pray for?
what for? I don't know what for, for anything, what's the difference—what for?

Well you don't believe, she said. so what,
I won't ask for anything, I will simply pray
somehow, just so I can do the same thing you're doing, you know what I mean?

if they leave your number, I will call it,
but if I can't—what's left?

I know why everything turned out like this for us—
too much dependence on dictionaries,
on lexemes, and all those diphthongs that dissolve on the tongue,
the trust placed in them is not justified;
my language, I know, my dictionary,
is printed on bitter cream paper
that I read in bars and on trains,
which was bought on sale in East Berlin,
way back in the nineties when I didn't know you,
I will die a patriot, even if
you abandon this country forever,
I will try to call your number,
even if only voices from hell echo there,
I will keep paging through my fucking dictionary, even if
there isn't a single
unused word left.

nothing can hold her back
no one can talk her out of this
almost a hundred thousand words and phrases
but there's no talking to her

SOCIALISM

Slow summer, endless, and some days are like young
blades of grass capable of totally changing their structure by tensing
their filaments; the sky stretches over the railroad, bits of news fly by—
on such days I always remember an old friend, we used to play on the same
team; he was about twenty years older than me,
in his day he was invited to join one of the
"major league" teams in a warm harbor town in what was then the Soviet Union;
he would have played for sailors, the sports club would have covered everything;
    in the evening
he would have strolled on the city beach—an idol for sunburned boys;
however, for some reason he turned down the offer, became involved in black
    marketeering, sold hash,
and even spent a year in jail, someone had set him up, he said, but
personally I never believed that—hash, you know;
they let him out at the end of the eighties and he wound up playing on amateur
teams which he also trained; that's when we met,
and for some reason I still think of him often.

You know, he would often say, the Soviets taught me
to keep it simple, in terms of myself; it's enough to choose
only those bits you need; you want to know why I turned
them down? simply because I thought it really made no difference—to play or
not to play, there was no difference, you know?
my career? well, I can still play, but the hash, you know?

I constantly have flashbacks on the field, otherwise I'm fine;
obviously I understood little then, but now
I think, truly there was reason to be tempted—
the sunny eighties in the big country, black marketeering was wrecking the Soviets,
communism, pop music, and Yugoslavia,
he still looks pretty good now, except for the flashbacks
during games, otherwise—he's fine, a pretty good master of his sport,
as he should be.

It's a bad habit to lug around all kinds of garbage from the past,
things you don't need; at some point you stop
and understand that you can't carry all that grief and joy,
life offers you too many temptations, this life is too tempting a trick—
just short enough to be told in one sitting
and too depressing to share with others;
every summer it's the same thing—you don't understand
whether you gained or lost more;
and everything continues incredibly,
but even water will eventually heat up
from the rhythmic beating
of the malleable hearts of fish.

OCEANS

Suddenly, it feels like there's a lot of water
maybe because each snow drifts and smells like the ocean,
then the presence of something great appears in your life;
everything was created counting on your heartbeats,
no wonder these waves, unseen and unheard,
turn toward people.

They can't be confined to their assigned
territories, so at some point for a moment they run
into our dreams, like children running into their parents' bedroom.
And even if you can't see them, this does not mean
that they cannot be seen.

That part of living
which we call life
could never contain that many sounds.
You say, silence, knowing that silence is exactly
what you cannot hear.

There are basements,
there are roofs,
and somewhere in between the ocean is hidden; and all you see—
the wet winter trees, rivers,
and grass—

is in its own world like
joy or parting is in ours.

So sometime near dawn,
they start rolling in but stop just short,
like someone pulling out a knife next to your face
or like a printing press punching out
                              letters with warm blood
on the other side of wrapping paper,
and in the window a bird flies so slowly,
that I can see it
as I write these necessary words
and then cross them out.

HEMP HARVESTERS

When they finally broke up,
he started receiving odd postcards from her;
look, she wrote, these are hemp harvesters,
they return to town carrying
warm plants on their backs,
they walk into their buildings carefully
stepping over turtles and old
newts blind with age;

every morning reeds grow through the earthen floor
of their buildings and are made by shepherds
into strange wind instruments whose sounds differ
with the direction of the wind;

and driving out their herds in the morning, they
send ahead paper dragons and
wave long bamboo poles
awakening orange stars from their dreams,

saying—

forward, you ancient warrior turtles, forward march,
untangle yourself from this thick grass, crush the emerald leaves; behind us our
children will definitely follow our voices, they will reach the end of these

endless fields, where we will die of fever and old age, so

forward, forward march, to the call of paper dragons, to the movement of night
   animals, to the shadows of the dead, who cannot push through this thick
   grass.

Look, she wrote him,
   everything that happened and everything that will happen,
   things that stand in your way or strengthen you—
   all this is in the hands of strangers who do the dirty work;
   our grand reality with its cafés
   and banks actually waits for your
   awakening every morning;

everything lives when you are present,
   everything ends when you die,
   all this will never cease,
   all this continues forever
   without beginning or end
   till death.

History of Culture at the
Turn of This Century (2003)

To Live Means to Die

I didn't know where any of her friends lived,
where her mother lived, where her lovers lived.
I went back to my court and wrote some love poems.
—Charles Bukowski, from the novel *Women*

HISTORY OF CULTURE AT THE TURN OF THIS CENTURY

You will reply today touching the warm letters,
sorting through them in the dark, confusing consonants with vowels,
like a typist in an old Warsaw office.
The honeycombs glisten
heavy with the gold from which language is spun.
Don't stop, just write,
type over the empty white space, stomp through the silent black trail.
No one will return from the long night walks,
and snails will die forgotten on wet grass.

Central Europe lies under tissue-white snow.
I always believed in the lazy movements of Gypsies,
not everyone has inherited this worn coin.
If you look at their passports
which smell of mustard and saffron,
if you hear their worn-out accordions
which reek of leather and Arabian spices,
you'd hear them say that when you leave — no matter where you go —
you only create more distance and are never closer than you are now;
when the songs of old gramophones die,
a residue seeps out
like tomatoes
from damaged cans.

The overburdened heart of the epoch bursts every morning,
but not behind these doors, not in cities burned by the sun.
Time passes, but it passes so near that if you
look closely, you can see its heavy warp,
and you whisper overheard sentences
as if you wanted someone someday to recognize your voice and say,
this is how the era began,
this is how it turned—awkward, heavy like a munitions truck,
leaving behind dead planets and burnt-out transmitters,
scattering wild ducks in the pond
that fly off and call louder
than the truckers,
god,
barges.

When choosing your course of studies you should find out
among other things
                    if the culture at the turn of this century
has already pressed itself into the veins of your lazy arm,
rooted itself in the whorls of your thick hair
carelessly blown by the wind
                    and tousled by fingers
like warm water in a basin,
like a fringe of colored beads over cups and ashtrays,
like the vast autumn sky
over a cornfield.

THE SELL-OUT POETS OF THE '60S

The sell-out poets of the '60s should be happy
that everything turned out as well as it did;
after all, there were many dangerous moments;
but see — they survived, paid their debts,
their battle wounds
only ache during storms,
like monthly cramps.

The sell-out poets of the '60s drag
huge suitcases made of fake yellow leather,
stay in hotels,
hold phone receivers with their shoulders like violins,
and their suitcases are covered with stickers.
Girl, the Viet Cong are our collective unconscious.
You don't really care about me — you'll throw away my crumpled phone number.
One more visa in my passport,
one less.

One day stuck in a snowed-in airport,
one of them will remember the lectures they gave,
Berlin radio and bridges over the Wisła River.
"Those were good," he'll think, "good
times, not bad — our sell-out '60s,
too bad afterward there was so much
masturbation and social democracy on the brain.

Love led us,
love ripped the tonsils from our throats,
like they rip receivers from pay phones.
Poetry is written with the throat
but this throat is constantly hoarse."

According to all the rules of literature,
according to all the stipulations in the contracts they signed,
they truly fought for freedom,
and freedom, as we know, demands
that we fight for her once in a while —
in trenches, forests,
and on the pages of an independent press.

Speaking of poetry,
let us remember all those who remained
on the streets and beaches of the good old '60s,
all those who did not pass the rehabilitation course,
and to this day clouds hang over them,
their structure reminiscent of American free verse;
let us remember them since what you call time
is a slaughterhouse
where guts are spilled simply because
this is the place to do it;
and only the sell-out poets
survive,
with lungs blown out
by love.

SERBO-CROATIAN

The Serbian girl crosses the street
avoiding the autumn bazaar and its hanging merchandise.
She notices that this fall there's plenty of gold in the vegetables and kerchiefs—
the warm onion is so golden;
there's a lot of light in the restaurants,
where portraits of Franz Joseph
hang on the walls.

The warmth of this autumn touches you too,
and so does this young woman who searches for something in her backpack,
pulling out her phone and pencils and placing them on the table;
you'll have your winter yet,
you'll have your dreams,
but the sky grows heavier every autumn
and the devil
grabs sinners
like sugar plums
in brightly colored wrappers.

Bitter Slavic syntagmas—
she tells you she bought envelopes in the tobacco store,
and walked to the subway,
and the doves flew down and beat against her like rain;
because of her tale, no one notices the sun has set,

they only notice that her cheeks
have grown somewhat darker.

Try to explain to her
that if you don't collect
the autumn clocks in time
they simply grow overripe and squirt
juice on your clothes and hands
later attracting bees
that pierce their stingers
straight into your heart.

CLEANING LADIES IN THE CORRIDORS

The old cleaning ladies in the corridors
slowly scrape the floors like ship decks;
do you hear, they're whispering about something in the stairway,
fearfully hugging the walls;
using long hooks, they pull out
water rats and bitter dreams.

The rooms all round are loaded with shadows,
like battleships filled with coal;
the cleaning ladies in the corridors
scrape fish scales with sharp knives,
shove huge tapestry needles into the morning sun;
the end of autumn approaches
and the skies are so dark it's as if someone's piled up
cut-off chicken heads
and black roses.

When they wash off the fish blood,
they gather at the train station, drink warm wine,
and talk about
how today fish lose their way in the Danube
and can't swim into the shallows

without the help of night lanterns
on ships,
without voices from the shore,
without openings and tunnels
in the damned ice.

POLISH ROCK

Falling asleep, she remembered the river—
somewhere in the caverns of sleep, where she started to forget his face,
the freezing river glistened bronze from its center,
                          although snow covered its current;
later old postwar locomotives crawled out of the mist
and workers came out in their blue denim overalls.

We wound up on opposite sides of winter,
and the announcer's voice, caught in a random taxi
reminds you
of the eighties when the radio
was full of Polish rock:
rock 'n' roll—mechanics in train depots listened to it,
rock 'n' roll flew over the Carpathian Mountains,
leaking into the air somewhere near Rava-Ruska;
our country is not big enough for us to miss each other,
our air space is not vast enough
for us to listen to different kinds of music.

I think that if a direct link to God existed
it would be through the help of
                 warm brown covers
containing Polish rock records
with narrow grooves cut by God's nails

on their black fields;
you can see his vinyl skin,
you can feel his strawberry blood,
washing off the dust and
wiping the cuts
with a sponge soaked in vinegar.

Birds frightened by the wind
calm down and assume their places
in the spaces between her heartbeats,
without knowing what she sees in her sleep,
or who she is forgetting in the middle of the dry river bottom;
her life's baggage—beauty marks on her skin and
tram tickets in her jacket pockets;
soon winter will roll from one hill onto the next,
and the hot weather will come,
when so many things grow from the earth
that the air has to rise a little higher
to avoid touching the long tall stems
that grow out of nowhere and stretch toward nowhere
just beneath her window.

PRIMARY SCHOOL

This has started up again for the zillionth time,
but I'm talking as if I'm seeing her for the first time —
everything is like it always was, but today the wind
is freezing in the mailboxes
and copper coins ring sadly
in matchboxes.

You're simply approaching that time of your life
when you start dreaming of people your age,
as if time ran backward, searching for something.
How many of those ever-hungry wolf cubs are still alive?
All their journeys to nowhere
usually started on main streets,
to end up watching life from the windows of bus stations,
to die on a never-ending road.
Ten years ago you, too,
used someone else's
shampoo so often
that your hair at times lost
its own smell.

And now dreams break off
in your body like long-distance conversations
on buses in July,

their seats smelling of sandalwood and St. John's wort
as you return to your town,
where every summer you find
rusty blades in the bathroom
and soda machines in the street.

What has changed? The trees have grown,
the old movie houses have disappeared
and so have dairy shops.
Only rainwater remains as sweet,
especially on apples,
which grow heavy
and fall down, down onto the ground,
smashed to bits
under the burning sky.

TO LIVE MEANS TO DIE

In summertime when wedding rings and fingernails
grow warm on men in hotels near train stations,
and children from the projects hug black soccer balls
close to their hearts in the shadows;

the rosé goes flat in the wineries at dusk
as the train to Budapest crawls snail-slow under the moon,
fragile like crumbling hot rocks.

Dying once, you continue your journey
through the yards at night and notice
death holds out mint candies in its hand
to children in empty lots near the station.

In summertime when life's warm lining is turned inside out,
when the small cars the color of your lip gloss crash,
the old pharmacist who cures everyone with an aspirin daily
plays some mysterious game with death;
life does not start without you—women laugh in the square,
to live means to die, you're told by lonely couriers
who carry dry heavens in their backpacks.

Dying once, you step into the shadows,
watch your body helplessly search

for itself in the thick leaves of grass;
dying during the summer,
the souls of the dead break the lines
strung up by postmen and like clinging vines
cut their own verticals through the air.

When you learn how, try to tear me free
from the internal night of this country,
free from the invisible heavenly portals
through which love comes to us.

Who will stop you, girl, who will drive out
the insects and spirits in your body?
The land I share with you under the summer sky
smells so fragrantly of moon and bandages each summer.

. . . After death as you step aside,
you will see the seam in the air through which
secret technicians project
a film of the great heavens
on your body,
so that the souls of the dead
and emerald shadows of beetles
fly into its light . . .

POST OFFICE

With the post office in the slow thaw
and the morning department stores filled with pizza delivery boys,
you easily grab the things you need daily:
the pipe with hashish
and the cup of tea,
the thick mug covered with honey—
you avoid drafts and correspondence;

a view of the city, fallen silent,
the street trade is not very lively at this hour,
two or three vendors with roasted chestnuts
look at the sky,
and the snow is falling, but so aimlessly
that it melts before it reaches the
flocks of birds;

and so the birds play—
overhead there's so much snow,
but it's so empty under their wings
that they want to fly endlessly under low bridges,
catching the smell of roasting chestnuts in their beaks;

everyone can find something, if they only look carefully,
angels pour coarse sand and diamonds under your feet,
the sun is so helpless in the middle of winter,
all it can do is simply move —
from East to West, dear,
from East to West.

ELEGY FOR URSULA

Boats loaded with Spanish garlic
enter the port after a long voyage home,
encrusted with barnacles like false gold.
I know—last night
dry sheets reeked of
sailors' overalls and tar till dawn;
stars fell on the shore like never before
and boats, evading buoys,
ran between your fingers till you woke up.

What did you see before you died?
The constant stream of air doesn't allow
you to stop breathing, and your constant breath
doesn't allow you to pause as you cross the border.
What can you see at the end
when you are about to die?
Somewhere in the north an iceberg formed,
as the innermost parts of the heart
grew cold at dawn and froze.
Did you notice the snow in the mouths
of fish jumping out of the water?
And did you recognize the river
that flows below the rocky landscape
resembling a pile of heavy wet
sheets?

At twenty-eight
I remember so many names
which no one mentions in the present tense anymore,
so many names which when pronounced
fill the mouth with blood and snow.
I don't know if I dare talk about you in this way;
I think death is like walking from one
empty room into another
creating a gust that rips out the electrical sockets
and chills the blood of those who remain.

And brave young birds with weather-beaten hearts,
waves on northern lakes that remain neck deep
because they don't dare roll onto the shore,
tall trees deprived of leaves, like citizenship:
return to the place where time's lackluster pearls harden on eyelashes,
where sweet tobacco and seaweed grow on sand,
where every morning cabin boys from sunken ships gather
without betraying their flags or finding peace,
and over them soar the souls
of mangled oranges.

Chinese Cooking

Warm beer and cold women . . .
—Tom Waits, from the album *Nighthawks at the Diner*

CHINESE COOKING

This happened some fifteen years ago, if I'm not mistaken.
Right here, you know, on the next street, there's a tall building
where they rent out rooms,
well, several Chinese lived there then and, it turned out, they were trafficking
    drugs in their own stomachs
like some unseen heavenly caviar, capable of finally destroying this rotten
    civilization.

These rooms were mostly rented out by taxi drivers and charlatans,
as well as aeronauts, deprived of their heavenly apparatus, who always made
    coffee in the kitchen
and listened to jazz radio stations
till things would start to glow with a bright light without casting shadows
while former rugby players drank beer and smoked camels as they played cards
    and talked about their damned rugby.

But something went wrong with the Chinese business, much was written about
    this later,
you know how it is: one day the split wasn't right, and that was it—
so they had this terrible shoot-out right there in the backyard,
scaring rats into the basement and birds into the heavens.

I stop in there once in a while; I make a little detour on my way home,
I look up at the fire escapes and see the sky in which, if you think about it,
   there's nothing but sky,
and you know, sometimes it seems to me that people really die
because their hearts stop out of love for this
strange-strange fantastic world.

CHILDREN'S TRAIN

Get out of the rainy street into the auditorium,
in March when many of the city's insane
warm themselves in libraries and free public toilets,
turning their brown eyes to the light like newts;
the generous hand of time dips into its watery reservoirs
and pours into your palms
handfuls of mussels and snails,
comets and river rocks.

There was a time when all the train stations in my city
stopped like alarm clocks
with a thousand broken springs;
hiding beneath the sky
in which two lights flew
like a person with two hearts;
red-haired girls who held dusk on the tip of their tongues,
sang a song of coal
full of old armor, clothes, and decaying tarantulas;
and on the hill where the city ended,
you could see the train
the workers took home.

In this mining village,
so much fire, tears, and coal

burned in the lungs, sails full of wind.
Why does the sky gather all the sweets,
goods, and light
only to turn its back and disappear behind the hill?

We paid with our lives
for every invisible exhaled breath of each butterfly exhausted by the night,
for every orphan folding his sheets like a parachute in the morning,
for every clarinet stuck in your throat which won't let you breathe,
transforming the voice into shadows and jazz into disease.
Hold me tighter. The experience
you gain is a scaffold
to support unsteady young lungs
with wire and chalk.

And the snow like old sheets
stuffed in the dresser drawers of heaven
won't cover your grief. Look—
gusts dance from border to border
and train stations like unexploded bombs crouch in the dark,
and lonely night express trains like lake serpents
swim through the dark, beating their tails
around your heart.

HOTEL BUSINESS

In cheap Berlin hotels run by Russians
there are no candies in the lobby or in the rooms—of course—
no envelopes with the hotel's logo,
tubs yellow with age
hide fish and scorpions;
the frequent guests have seen life
and have many tales to tell before they collapse
into bed with their liquor and old cigarette holders.

While they talk and chew the sliced ham
bought in the store across the street,
the ash from their cigarettes falls on the bed,
snow on a port city,
the moon manages to move from the street corner closer to the church,
and the cleaning ladies start their morning rounds
to find condoms in showers
and towels smeared with blood.

One day a man takes a room
in one of these hotels; he shows his student ID
to register and locks himself in his room.
In the morning they bring him breakfast, and he
takes the tray, then, without taking off his clothes or shoes,
gets into the tub and turns on the water.

The cleaning ladies gossip about this endlessly
since they found him the next day
and called the police.
Did he have to swallow so many sleeping pills
just to drown in the tub?
See, death can smell of
Turkish coffee,
and what should we do after this?

Cities torn apart by the cravings of lonely women,
the moon covered with the saliva of young immigrants—
everything they talk about, all the stories they have to tell,
every gulp and every puff,
is only an excuse to continue the endless conversation.

Few guess at the limits of the visible world,
especially in this room with its toaster and night light,
from which there is no return and no explanation;
you will not listen to the frightened cleaning lady
who first entered the room
and saw the wet currency and black dolphins
float in the water
as spiders and angels descended
from the ceiling on thin webs
to throw rose petals
into the chlorinated water.

USED CAR SALESMAN

In 1980 when Tito died
high up in the salad-green sky of Europe,
the flywheels that helped heat up the ore and silver
in the mines near our borders stopped for a moment.
It was a great time, a great era, that gave birth to heroes;
now you wander through a foreign country,
stop near a basketball court,
watch teens poke at the sky
with metal rods trying
to get it to move along.

> A fight we once lost
> doesn't mean anything to anyone else;
> in Irish bars male fingers
> touch piano keys,
> as they sing a hymn to easy homelessness.

> Every key's
> another sound,
> fingers strain to make the instrument
> say something more
> about our love
> and torment.

Now fat heats up in smoky kitchens
and cooks chop submissive greens with sharp knives,
Now women in dresses the color of hearts and hot sauce
disappear into the shadows of the yard;
the Lord gave us our borders,
our anger and bravery, as well as our cocaine,
and now I worry every time
I go to communion or transfer
bucks from one bank
to another.

So play this happy melody to its end:
we once met
under a starlit sky,
and now we are frightened
because our sky contains
fewer and fewer
stars.

NONCOMMERCIAL FILM

In one photo I found in the apartment
that I'm renting there is a girl,
13–14, in a revealing bathing suit
on some beach near a rocky cliff;
the girl looks straight at the camera as if to say, "Greetings,
you nerds, it's me," and underneath someone wrote "Bucharest '86," so now
she's just under thirty, more or less my age—that is,
if she hasn't dropped dead in her Bucharest from drinking,
which isn't curable in Bucharest, or here for that matter.

Oddly enough, I've been thinking of that time—what mush
filled our brains then! All that intellectual masturbation of the seventies,
those tales about the beats and lefty professors, about freedom of consciousness
and new jazz, which was supposed to be revived by white folks and other nonsense;
so now fifteen years have passed, and you can only gather
random testimony about those earth-shattering events and little-known
contemporaries, scattered all over the land, who if they didn't die of
communism or syphilis now hold history by the throat in their own lands
and are not willing to forgive history for its disgusting sell-outs, and rightly so—
angels should have thought three times before getting involved
with those clowns—they're at fault and now must pull them out of their depression
and buy prayer books, but we're only repeating what
happens in heaven, and what is heaven, if not a hall
of mirrors angled in such a way that, of course, you
can't see anything.

Everything depends on the weather and the time of year—living in the capitals
of old Europe filled to the brim with fresh immigrant meat,
you must decide what you should really do; for instance
you can walk into a small movie house on a side street far from
the center of town where they still show real old movies,
the torn seats occupied by a few senior citizens
and perverts watching those eternally young girls
whose faces they first saw in their youth,
and then you can go home to your apartment, where
every year there's less and less air, and there are
more and more demons, who gather around your bed at night
when you fall asleep, carefully examining the tattoos on your arms
and commenting on the most interesting patterns
by quoting Saint Augustine.

FUNERAL ORCHESTRA

Stories connected with murders, knife wounds,
suicides, botched abortions—in general,
stories connected with crime—interest
people because they're parables. In these stories
men are manly and dutiful while children
braid roses of the Lord's omniscience
into their hair. In these stories
death always runs ahead, wanting to see
how it all ends; many people like the fact
that in these stories death begins in life
so you can glance into its adolescent
face.

In such stories sooner or later there appear musicians
who play funeral marches: they jump out of a dilapidated
bus onto the grounds of the cemetery and pull out
bagpipes, trombones, and hunters' horns from under their coats, roll out
drums and hurdy-gurdies, and blow great cemetery jazz
over the deceased, the bloody unrestrained music of despair
and disobedience, heart-wrenching gangster melodies, melodies of old
tunes popular with sailors and prostitutes,
and then everyone who came to see the deceased on his last
journey starts to breathe easier because these are the rules,
this is the ritual, or something like that; in a word
they're not afraid of the dead but of becoming one of them.

Also, as a rule, there are women in these stories,
they deserve a separate discussion—those
forty-year-old women who still display
the passion and indecisiveness of seventeen-year-old girls;
they cry about every senseless life spent on such
trivialities as love and faith, they remember how
the great depression began in our country
and still whisper the words
that were said to them in parting:

> *everything is okay, girl, drugs won't help me now,*
> *I want to love you more than you want to have children,*
> *life has not stopped as we assumed, see—in the morning*
> *couriers will arrive from the train station and lovers will part*
>   *on the stairs as usual,*
> *I will stay with you, watch*
> *when praying mantises sit in your palm and move over your*
> *sleeping body, send them patience, heavens,*
> *on their journey without end.*

ALCOHOL

The green river water
slows in warm bends
fish zeppelins
scatter the plankton
and tired bird catchers
attempt to catch
every word.

Hold on to
the brightly colored rags and scotch tape
that bind the slashed wrists
of these heroic times.
One day you will turn off this radio,
you'll get used to her,
to her breathing,
and, dressed in your T-shirt,
she'll bring you water in the middle of the night.

On the terrace the leftover cups of tea
are filling up with rainwater
and cigarette butts;
you and I share a cold,
you and I share long conversations —
you don't notice the morning rain,

you go to sleep late
and you wake up late.
I write poems about how I love
this woman, and I invent
newer and newer words
to avoid
telling her.

Children's Crusade

Their children will not speak Spanish
or kneel in any Christian church.
—William S. Burroughs, "The Revised Boy Scout Manual"

CHILDREN'S CRUSADE

You hear everything passing,
you hear everything remaining,
now everything has somehow stopped, you understand, your world and your personal
jesus, with you in those times that were not your best,
now silently leave, since everything exists only as long as
you look at it, here—look—it's already next summer,
that same season again,
and so you remember
those who were alive this time last year,
those who knew that they were sick,
those who suspected
death might be near.

The constant visions of the dead at five in the morning in the stairway—
dreams of faces of TV anchors;
death usually comes during those
silent mornings carrying the smell
of wet vegetables and iodine.

Children can see death
in the empty-empty streets of my city
filled with the silent-silent voices of birds that have grown deaf living near highways,
as they die alone in urban nests.

You simply learn to write,
you learn to write simply,
trying not to forget even one of those insanely beautiful
enchanting homeless children who passed by you unnoticed during
your life on your neighborhood
streets.

You listen to all that remains,
you listen but don't know what to do with their things,
with their guileless treasures
marked with nail polish and
the sweet filth of the street.
Your memories exist as long as you want to remember them,
not a moment longer,
when you leave your building and keep walking, that's how far
you will have to return.
Not one step farther,
not one step less.

They never knew fear in their endless street dealings,
they never hesitated to cross the border
where the great damned emptiness begins,
they simply walked through life, moving
from one brightly lit window to the next.

But now you see our
drums and flags are transforming
and our heavens are being cleansed of all the unrepentant souls

who used to fill them;
how worn their battle clothes and boots,
and has that little boy's leather jacket been worn out
by wings or
a gun strap?

Do you hear how they respond
from the other side between four and five in the morning?
Their voices can be mistaken for
the calls of milkmaids at dawn or
the outbursts of drunken thieves.

Silently touching the air from the other side of death,
silently-silently moving your lips—
how many words can you say, how many can you pronounce,
so many more will remain stuck in your
throat, interrupting your breathing,
burdened with their bitterness; one day you will simply
fall silent, not able to add anything more,
you will simply cease, without saying good-bye—
they whisper but all that is left
in the stairwells is the smell of iodine,
the smell of death.

Holding one another by the hand,
so close they can't breathe,
in dreams losing consciousness from love and
malnutrition,

they fill the air of our cities
with mist and flying beetles.

Never before and never after,
will anyone under any circumstances
so easily escape from this life,
as they have,
like fish jumping out of water after their
prey.

Do you hear? Fish, fish that smell of iodine
and swim to shore,
awaiting death, but then return,
and their smell reminds you
of the smell of crucifixes on the dashboards of trucks which
deliver bits of the great European emptiness
down river,
it is the smell of pharmacies, the smell
of christ's gills on the truckers' catholic crosses
and the orange color
of the truckers' nails.

As this happened, as waves overlapped,
beating their salty tails on the corrugated metal roofs
of buildings built in the fifties,
the ocean rolled into young souls
drunk for the very first time;

in cities, where public drinking fountains
are filled to the brim with rainwater and vomit,
in street bazaars
trained angels
walk on red-hot coals like in the circus,
nothing else could have happened
since these cities were
in the hands of villains, of deserters,
demons and shapeshifters who hid in our
childhood closets;

they couldn't do anything else,
and had to cover this up,
gathering children under banners
and giving them maps
to roads
that don't
exist.

Answering every horn in the orchestra
of the dead,
happily banging on cardboard props
and hiding road gravel
black and hard like
hockey pucks in their pockets—
these children could've gotten to the sea eventually
and, cutting across it, wound up somewhere

in a much more blessed land
where the sky is low and clear,
where you can feed seagulls and wild bees from your hand,
but look at their tracks and you will understand:

every children's crusade
ends
when the children simply grow up
and go home—
without finally counting the dead,
without noticing those who have
no home to return to;

only police helicopters
beat their tails
through the roadside sky.

That is why you listen as people enter
the streets in the morning.
They chat so happily in this space
with their personal jesus, holding him by the gills
and placing wet vegetables in their baskets;

the silent-silent voices of those
who returned from their crusade
and are now afraid to tell anyone
how horrid real time can be—
the tired, insane creature who runs across

your path on the sandy shore
and eats bread and chocolate from your hand,
the tired-tired being that is destined
to constantly run after circus wagons,
leaving town and moving
down river
toward Palestine.

What passes and what is retained as memory—
programs from soccer matches and porn flicks,
circus ads where gymnasts resemble
uncanonized saints;

learn to just look at children,
just listen to news,
just be awake,

and from street vendors
and in supermarkets
buy cold
wet
cabbage
in memory of all the dead.

Ballads About War and Reconstruction (2001)

MUSIC FOR THE FAT

in the home for senior citizens yuri andrukhovych
is a seventy-year-old cranky writer
    the author of half-forgotten detective novels
cared for by the city and the writers union
    with a mountain of obsessions
with moths in his pajama pockets
beaded bracelets on his knotty wrists
razors and forks scattered around the room
he adjusts the hands of the clock to autumn
    exhales and listens to this voice-over:
salman rushdie—indian
yuri andrukhovych—ukrainian
if you haven't screwed up
the poetry of your nation can be understood by others
without translation
even if you don't give a shit

thirty years without war
thirty years without a future
thirty years of old-time music

    writing into the void
    in a country with agricultural oomph
here are your suitcases

your kidneys
your literature

when you're past sixty-four
when your blood slows down and has to think
where it should flow next
here
yes
here
the sewing machine of the universe cries till dawn
spinning its tired mechanisms
not stopping
for even a moment

so morning comes to the windows of the home for senior citizens
and the sky is brown after the rain
and fish lie on the frying pan like
lovers on a hot august bed
and yuri andrukhovych known to everyone by sight here
looks through yesterday's papers and
          highlights his own name with a marker
          highlights the ideas he likes
          highlights the names of friends who have died
          highlights interesting radio shows
                    for the coming week

a bunch of words and passersby
only a dachau left of this whole generation

and walking out for breakfast
later
he notices among other things:
the warm air
the dry air
too bad there are no birds
but there were never any
in this barrack

NEW YORK FUCKIN' CITY

as if water wasn't pouring down
growing cold on the cement knocking people off their feet
just tossing me down on the sidewalk
to arrhythmic music and blissful heavens
I know—it's hard to learn anything from experiences like these
a roadside wasp flies by the window heading south
as an independent radio station announces
that you're approaching the city

when the weather turns bad
there's no luck or peace, although both were promised
a young transvestite emerges from around the corner
in a long raincoat and a warm skirt
stops at the front door looking for keys rain pouring down her face
the makeup cakes under her eyes like dirt under nails
great blue drops run down her narrow cheeks
onto woolen clothes and black boots

as if indeed no trace remained
and memory wasn't water and wasn't growing cold deep inside the body
love of large cities
is like the love of trees that grow without you
you say to yourself as you imperceptibly fall asleep
and your eyes roll up behind the lids
like lost toys

THE END OF UKRAINIAN SYLLABOTONIC VERSE

they once lived in this building
see the fading red paint blistering on the window frames
it's from those times when someone decided to put
them all into one building so that their breath could be heard
                                        in the hallways
breath like wind structured in fear
                        as you look in the yard
you can see soldiers laying asphalt
and planting pines

>   they were led out at night their dreams scattering
>   from their shoulders like rats from windowsills
>   their gray shirts were soaked with sweat
>   and yellow piss hid in their bodies
>   like contraband
>   those who led them out enjoyed the scent
>   of the night scene
>   gray underwear wet with sudden awakening
>   women with their faces smeared
>   with makeup and fear

at the corner newsstand there's warm lemonade
and sticky violet drops of syrup that pull your skin
and stick to your fingers and lips

bees brush against your clothing and eyelashes with their heavy tails
and the shadow of the building creeps up to your feet
like a great flood

if only you could get home sooner and shut the door tight
turn the heavy black lock and fasten the chain
listen to the wind rattling the doorjamb
and with your cheek
feel the sun beat
against the bare window

> *they were led out*
> *quickly through the street*
> *before the black automobiles swallowed them*
> *so for a moment they were still breathing oxygen*
> *the oxygen of the building, holding it*
> *trying not to let out*
> > *the smallest drop of freedom*
> *the smallest drop of hysteria*

when you decide to separate words
into those you used at least once and those you've never touched
you will feel the silence that ripped apart
the heart of that night—the tortured circle
you sense each time you return to this place

because long ago fragments of hot lexemes
grew cold in mouths filled with fear

and the man with the serious expression
and his dark notebook and wooden pencil
left behind only silence
                that fell like a dead bird

it's simple, such buildings exist
where the final border is particularly grim
where hell and the veins of underground ore are unexpectedly close
where time sticks out like lumps of coal from the ground
where death begins and where literature ends

TRANSLATOR'S NOTE ON "THE END OF UKRAINIAN SYLLABOTONIC VERSE"

The building in the poem is the Slovo (Word/Logos) building. It was built in the late 1920s as a luxury apartment building for the cultural elite of Kharkiv, then the capital of Ukraine. All the great Ukrainian writers were living in the Slovo in 1930. But starting in May 1933, the arrests began, one by one, usually in the middle of the night. The authorities had targeted the intelligentsia as dangerous dissidents. The other residents of the building would hear the nightly disturbances and know that their time was coming. Some, like Mykola Khvylovy, the most influential of the writers, who had convinced the others to work with the government, chose suicide. Khvylovy shot himself on May 13, 1933, when he heard of a friend's arrest. Most residents kept a packed bag at hand with their essentials for prison. Because of the numerous arrests, people joked that the authorities should spare themselves the trouble and just put bars in the windows of the Slovo building. Many residents spent the next several years in prisons and work camps—and then were executed in the fall of 1937 as part of the government's "celebration" of the twentieth anniversary of the October Revolution.

This building conjures up strong emotions for me. I first saw it in December 1990, when I visited it in the company of an elderly actor. As we stood in the muddy courtyard, he pointed out the windows where various poets and artists had lived, including the theater director who was the topic of my thesis at Columbia University. I realized that everyone I wanted to talk to from that time had lived in this building. The experience profoundly changed the way I felt about contemporary Ukraine. Up till that moment I had found what I saw on this, my first trip, very hard to relate to. But that building spoke directly to me of another time, of exciting art and the high price that the artists who created it paid. I wanted people today to be aware of what they had done. Ten years later, when by chance I read "The End of Ukrainian Syllabotonic Verse" in Ukrainian, I knew I had to translate this poem and I knew I wanted to work with Zhadan.

Virlana Tkacz

ACKNOWLEDGMENTS

The poems listed below were first published in English in the following publications. Some translations have been modified slightly for this volume.

Anthologies

In a Different Light: A Bilingual Anthology of Ukrainian Literature Translated into English by Virlana Tkacz and Wanda Phipps as Performed by Yara Arts Group, ed. Olha Luchuk (Lviv: Sribne Slovo, 2008): "The End of Ukrainian Syllabotonic Verse"

Letters from Ukraine: Poetry Anthology (Lviv: Art Council "Dialogue"/Drohobych: KOLO Publishing House, 2016): "'Where Are You Coming From?'" "So I throw down my weapon and start to crawl" (published as "So I Throw Down My Weapon")

Modernism in Kyiv: Jubilant Experimentation (Toronto: University of Toronto Press, 2010): "The End of Ukrainian Syllabotonic Verse"

New European Poets, ed. Kevin Prufer and Wayne Miller (Saint Paul, Minn.: Graywolf Press, 2008): "Alcohol"

New York Elegies: Ukrainian Poetry on the City (Boston: Academic Studies Press, 2018): "New York Fuckin' City"

The White Chalk of Days: Contemporary Ukrainian Literature Series Anthology, ed. Mark Andryczyk (Boston: Academic Studies Press, 2017): "Chinese Cooking," "Hotel Business," "Alcohol," "Contraband," ". . . not to wake her up," "The Lord Sympathizes with Outsiders," "Neither the smallest girl in Chinatown" (published as "The Smallest Girl in Chinatown"), "Sweet Peppers" (published as "Paprika")

Words for War: New Poems from Ukraine, ed. Oksana Maksymchuk and Max Rosochinsky (Boston: Ukrainian Research Institute, Harvard University, with the Borderlines Foundation for Academic Studies and Academic Studies Press, 2017): "Take Only What Is Most Important"

Journals

Absinthe: New European Writing 7 (2007); www.absinthenew.com: "Serbo-Croatian," "Elegy for Ursula," "Used Car Salesman," "Hotel Business," "Children's Crusade"

Circumference: Poetry in Translation (Spring/Summer 2005); www.circumferencemag.com: "Noncommercial Film"

Consequence Magazine 8 (Spring 2016); www.ConsequenceMagazine.org.: "Take Only What Is Most Important"

Dekadentzya 2 (2010): "The Sell-Out Poets of the '60s" (published as "Sell-Out Poets of the '60s"), "Dictionaries in the Service of the Church"

International Poetry Review 36, no. 2 (Fall 2010): "Primary School"

Inventory 2 (Fall 2011): ". . . remember how winter began in your town," "Oceans," "Hemp Harvesters"

Mantis: A Journal of Poetry and Translation 6: Geographies (Summer 2007): "Music for the Fat"

National Endowment for the Arts Annual Report (2005): "Alcohol"

Two Lines: World Writing in Translation 14 (2007): ". . . not to wake her up"

Welcome to Ukraine 3 (Summer 2004): "History of Culture" and "Alcohol"

Wolf Magazine 23 (Summer 2010): "Alcohol"

Websites

The Madhatters Review 12: "To Live Means to Die," "Post Office," "Funeral Orchestra," "Socialism"

Napalm Health Spa Report 2004: "Serbo-Croatian," "Cleaning Ladies in the Corridor"

Poetry International Web — Ukraine: "Chinese Cooking," "Polish Rock," "History of Culture"

Poetry International Web, Rotterdam Festival: "Mushrooms of Donbas," "Lukoil," "Chinese Cooking," "Sweet Peppers" (published as "Paprika")

Translations in this book were performed as part of Yara Arts Group's theater pieces *Underground Dreams* (2014) and *Hitting Bedrock* (2015), as well as at numerous Yara festivals and art events. They were also part of artworks such as "Blind Spot," an installation by Mykola Rudnyi and Serhiy Zhadan at the 2015 Venice Biennale. www.brama.com/yara

Translations by Virlana Tkacz and Wanda Phipps were supported by public funds from the New York State Council on the Arts with the support of Governor Andrew M. Cuomo and the New York State Legislature. Virlana Tkacz was also awarded a National Endowment for the Arts Poetry Translation Fellowship for her work with Wanda Phipps on Serhiy Zhadan's poetry.

The translators would like to thank Svitlana Matviyenko, Sofia Riabchuk, Julian Kytasty, Olena Jennings, Kateryna Babkina and all the actors who worked on our poetry readings and theater shows for their assistance, especially Shona Tucker, Andrew Colteaux, Sean Eden, Meredith Wright, Marina Celander, Susan Hwang and Bob Holman.

SERHIY ZHADAN was born in the Luhansk Region of Ukraine and educated in Kharkiv, where he lives today. He is the most popular poet of the post-independence generation in Ukraine and the author of twelve books of poetry, which have earned him numerous national and European awards. His prose works include *Big Mac* (2003), *Depeche Mode* (2004), *Anarchy in the UKR* (2005), *Hymn of the Democratic Youth* (2006), *Voroshilovgrad* (2010), *Mesopotamia* (2014) and *The Orphanage* (2017). Zhadan's books have been translated into English, German, French, Italian, Swedish, Norwegian, Polish, Czech, Hungarian, Belarusian, Lithuanian, Latvian, and Russian. He is the front man for the band Zhadan and the Dogs.

VIRLANA TKACZ and WANDA PHIPPS have received the Agni Poetry Translation Prize, the National Theatre Translation Fund Award and twelve translation grants from the New York State Council on the Arts. Their translations have appeared in many literary journals and anthologies, and are integral to the theater pieces created by Yara Arts Group. www.brama.com/yara

WANDA PHIPPS is the author of the books *Field of Wanting: Poems of Desire* and *Wake-Up Calls: 66 Morning Poems*. She received a New York Foundation for the Arts Poetry Fellowship. Her poems have appeared in over one hundred literary magazines and numerous anthologies.

VIRLANA TKACZ heads the Yara Arts Group and has directed over thirty original shows at La MaMa Experimental Theatre in New York, as well as in Kyiv, Lviv, Kharkiv, Bishkek, Ulaanbaatar, and Ulan Ude. She received an NEA Poetry Translation Fellowship for her translations with Wanda Phipps of Serhiy Zhadan's poetry.

BOB HOLMAN is a poet, performer, and translator and the founder of the Bowery Poetry Club. He has performed with Serhiy Zhadan in New York and throughout Ukraine. He is a founder of the Endangered Language Alliance and host of *Language Matters* on PBS. www.bobholman.com